Owning a Positive Mindset

My Game Changer

T.Renee

ISBN 979-8-88644-774-3 (Paperback)
ISBN 979-8-88644-775-0 (Digital)

Covenant Books
11661 Hwy 707
Murrells Inlet, SC 29576
www.covenantbooks.com

"You never know how strong you are until *you*
are forced to face the inevitable—change."

—T.Renee

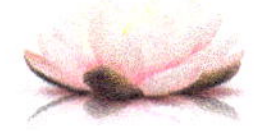

Acknowledgments

First and foremost, I want to give a huge shout-out, thanks, praise, and honor to my maker—the Alpha and Omega! The Lord and King of all Kings.

To my beautiful and gorgeous daughters, Brittany and Breana, and my handsome twin grandsons, Kingsley and Kenzo. You. all are my reason for living!

To my family that has continued to support and love me, thank you. There are too many of y'all to list.

To my die-hard, real sisters and friends, thank you so much for showing me love from another mother. You all know who you are!

To that special person in my life, thank you for loving me unconditionally, for accepting all my flaws, and for truly showing me *real love*!

Lastly, to the one who was led to purchase this book, may it plant seeds of greatness and awesomeness and affirm positive things in your life going forward. *Speak life*. "Blessed is she who has believed that the Lord would fulfill His Promises to her" (Luke 1:45).

Get Out of Your Own Way

You! Yes, *you*!

Is today the day you decide to get out of your own way?

What do you mean you say? I have so much going on. Not today. But when? Today nor tomorrow is not promised. So what do you say—step out of your comfort box and at least try today. But I'm scared. I'm not smart enough. I'm too old. I don't deserve better. I am not worthy. Who told you that? Why did you believe that? Don't *you* know whose are *you*? A one-of-a-kind creation deemed fit to see today's promise with the purpose of love and life. All you need is a little motivation, reassurance, focus, determination, and belief that *no weapon* will be formed against *you*! So plant those seeds of truth and goodness and not of doubt. Cancel all that negative energy out!

So what do you say… Let God lead the way, and just that easy, *you* decided that *today* was the day *you* got out of your way!

Contents

Plan

*You can't let your failures define you. You have to
let your failures teach you.—Barack Obama*

Process

*I can be changed by what happens to me. But I
refuse to be reduced by it.—Maya Angelou*

Progress

*You are the only real obstacle in your
path to fulfilling it.—Les Brown*

Manifest

*Be not afraid of growing slowly, be afraid
of standing still.—Chinese Proverb*

Plan

Chapter 1

When You Get the Wind Knocked Out of You

You can't let your failures define you. You
have to let your failures teach you.

—Barack Obama

Picture this scenario. Have you ever been sparring in the front yard or pillow fighting with your friends or siblings when you were a kid? Then suddenly, you get the living life or the *wind knocked out of you*?

Or so that's how it feels. It totally catches you off guard, and you don't even know how to respond.

Feelings rush in like a flood mad, hurt, and surprised? You're literally trying to catch your breath and bearings so that you can quickly get whoever hit you right back.

This is just an example of how we may feel when we get that unexpected surprise called "life happens." Situations and circumstances that literally catch us completely off guard, are unplanned, and definitely not scheduled.

It can be a situation where you lose a loved one suddenly or are fired from your longtime employment or your spouse of many years no longer wants to be in the marriage.

3

When life occurrences happen that make us pause, *stop*, readjust, refocus, or re-group on how we should deal or even respond, what processes do we have in place to help us manage and go through it?

Aren't you expecting nor prepared for any of this? In that split second, you go into either panic or strategic mode to figure out what to do next.

Situations in a split second can happen in changing one's dynamic. Nothing planned. It just happens totally out of your control. It's up to you to seek and develop a way of processing. Keep your peace of mind and attitude to embracing this sudden change.

We are never prepared for, nor do we want to think of the "what if" factor of any life-altering experience, especially when things seem to be going so well! So how do we coach ourselves on realizing and understanding strategies in advance to handle or maintain such?

Start by researching alternative methods and tools that will incorporate your growth, transition, conversion, and completion.

When going through any trial and tribulation, we must always keep in mind that in life, we go through a test. Sometimes you get the bitter with the sweet. Right now, you have now entered the testing phase. It's up to you how you will *plan, process, progress, manifest*, and create *success* from this outcome!

This sudden dilemma may have caught you off guard and knocked you down, but it is up to you to determine if it will keep you out of this game called life!

Engage in *prayer*, speak life, and mediate. Changing your mindset and surrounding yourself with positive people, places, and things. These practices are important and will aid greatly in your decision-making. Once all these things and systems are in place, together they can incorporate healing and give vision on embarking on your new journey.

Even when a plant is uprooted out of its soil, if the roots are strong, it will be replanted, thrive, and grow in the right element. Will it be easy? Probably not maybe even downright unbearable, but remember that any living thing when moved or shifted out of its comfort zone will adjust, it's in our nature.

Practice daily to AFFIRM, ACCEPT, ALLOW, and BELIEVE in yourself to go through, and trust the process of your new season. You will witness major growth and transformation.

This process will take time and hard work to master, but only YOU can complete this. In order to achieve ultimate success, continue to plant seeds of positivity, and learn to take time out to pour into yourself. Love yourself a little more during this time!

Allow your changing mindset to ease you through the toughest of times.

Have faith, be intentional with your energy, and know that this too shall pass!

Reflection: Have you ever experienced a situation or circumstances that caught you totally off guard? What were the tactics and tools you used to help you deal and achieve success?

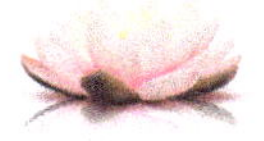

Chapter 2

When You Can No Longer Cheer in the Stands, Isolated, but Not Limited

I do not take constructive criticism from a
person who never constructed anything.
—Eric Thomas

The year 2020 has dictated the new norm—a new way of conducting events, activities, and even our plans that affect our daily way of life. Tasks that seemed so simple before the pandemic are no longer implemented nor suggested as such. The way we go about our day-to-day life and daily duties can be challenging and over the top.

When a quick errand to get milk from the grocery store used to be an easy task, now you must sanitize, and scan your body temperature, and you must be masked!

This vision seems like a scene straight out of a science fiction flick, but this indeed is our way of life as we know it today.

Everyone seemed to take notice of the seriousness of it all when children were not allowed to attend school and had to complete online classes for almost the entire school year.

Graduating via zoom, working remotely, or when sports fans were *no longer allowed to cheer in the stands?*

Staying at home and watching your favorite sports teams, which were also contained in a compound called "the bubble," was the new way to view and engage with your team.

Some would say, "Well, what's so bad about that? You miss standing in the long lines, the bumper-to-bumper traffic, and of course, the high cost of the tickets?" A die-hard, season-ticket holder looks forward to all of the above, in fact, it is almost downright ritualistic.

Before the season, preparation is essential. The energy and excitement from the atmosphere, arguing of the opposing sides, crowd participation, and tail-gate parties are the major elements that create the ultimate fan's game day experience.

This is what they look forward to year in and year out. So how do we learn to improvise when *we can no longer cheer in the stands?*

Planning is a particularly important tool that must be learned. Even though we all had to adjust, we still learned to acclimate quickly to function in our new routines.

Some of us may never master this technique in life, but adding tips and tricks to make this easier to master in our daily routines will allow us the ability to adapt and learn to change.

Take into consideration that we are always learning new ways to reform in our circumstances and situations. Gaining knowledge to alter and rescript our new mindset and procedures on how to accept the change of it.

The old way of thinking is no longer recognized or accepted. Implementing these practices surely takes time and patience, creating new methods in which you generate new techniques and systems.

Start by giving yourself daily goals to complete, weekly and then monthly. Continue to take part in the routines and rituals that you have created for yourself.

Daily *prayer*, affirmations, meditation, and taking time for *you*!

Slowly but surely, you will create new ideas, plans, and belief systems to encourage yourself to know *you* will win!

Nothing happens overnight, but when it is imperative, just like accepting the "new norm," the same can be implemented with your new routine of positive thinking, finding brand new ways to operate so that you can go back to cheering in the stands.

Reflection: How were you able to implement a "new norm"—a routine to help you maintain a positive mindset and forward thinking?

Chapter 3

No Thanks, Keep Your Fear? Second Guessing Due to Other's Experiences

Whatever you fear most has no power.
It is fear that has the power.

—Oprah Winfrey

We have all come across this particular topic in more ways than one. Coming from your momma, grandma, favorite aunt, your boss, or even your spouse, I'm sure one time or another you have experienced someone trying to put their past *fear* on *you* or place you in the same predicament they're currently in. Misery sure does love company.

The scenario goes something like this. You're telling others what you are about to undergo or encounter. Here they go, "Oh yes." I remember my niece did that exact same thing, and child, it was horrible. She didn't sleep for weeks, caught a rash, lost her appetite, and her jaw locked up. Your aunt Janice tried that same thing. Poor baby!

What? Get that negative thinking, disruptive seed planting, and discouraging words and mindset up out of here.

Did you know that negative words, especially spoken in anger, can cause significant damage to the brain?

They send alarming messages through the brain, which can cause interference with the decision-making center located in the frontal lobe. Negative words can even affect our personal vibration, the energy that we give and feel.

For example, you're excited about going after that promotion on your job, and you have taken the steps to gain training and get abreast with the new functions and processes for the position you are currently wanting to be promoted for. Or another example, after all the failed love relationships you have encountered, you are finally in a healthy and loving one. No matter which one you are experiencing, your new whatever… and here comes FEAR, their fear?

You get the negative experience pictured in your mind, and now it has converted to negative thinking and energy, and there goes all your confidence.

It has you literally wanting to run out into moving highway traffic, gone with no point of return. But what measures do we need to take to stop negative talking in its tracks?

If you can recall, you were so confident about your current situation. But because we value the opinions of the ones dearest and nearest to us, in an instance, we allow doubt to creep in.

If they've experienced the same thing, and for whatever reason, whether it wasn't *for them*, it is not their season or timing.

Their adverse effects from their experience can cause one to doubt their own decisions or make you feel not even worthy to encounter or enjoy it.

Wanting approval and acceptance of things or situations that we may consider to be the best choices is important to us. Allowing these negative influences can cause us to self-sabotage or lose out entirely on what was deemed for us.

How do we block the negative seeds that are unintentionally being planted? The same words we may receive from folks that genuinely love and care for us. "They just don't know any better," as my momma would say.

One, instantly stop them from speaking negative things about your existence. You do not have to accept nor agree with this. That's why it's so important to know your self-worth and what you possess! You embody the gifts and God-given talents to create and put forth greatness.

Two, find out what your purpose is. Step out and learn what this means to you. You control your destiny; things have already been aligned and waiting for you! We must have the faith to sometimes step out and trust no matter how intimidating that feat may be.

Three, get plenty of *rest* and eat healthy foods. Build your immune system. These things help in warding off being vulnerable when it comes to responses of any kind. *Affirm* positive quotes, write them down, and post them where you can see them daily. *Speak* to your inner man. Realize that you are *amazing*. Own it!

It is up to us not to receive the negative seeds that one tries to plant in our spirit of *their* experience. Unless you experience it for yourself, you will never know the true outcome.

Remember there is life and death in the power of the smallest thing on your body, which is the tongue (Proverbs 18:21).

It is up to you to sustain, plan, and process what will be implemented for *your* circumstance. Negative thinking does not have to be accepted by anyone. Period. "Umm, no thanks. You can keep that *fear*." Next.

Reflection: Use this time to implement new ideas or ignite old ones. Begin your planning phase to set new habits and intentions. ***You got this***!

Think of Goals
that you want to achieve...

Write them down with
INTENT...

CREATE
a Visual or Life-board...

Set a Timeframe for Goals
Daily, Weekly and Monthly...

Implement a list of
Daily Affirmations..

Maintain POSITIVE
Attitude and Surroundings...

Process

Chapter 4

When Situations Forces You into a Cocoon (Butterfly Effect)

I can be changed by what happens to me.
But I refuse to be reduced by it.

—Maya Angelou

Can you imagine being isolated and held up in one area for months without communicating or socializing with others, like family or friends, even in close proximity? Can you imagine being held up, which felt like being in a cocoon? It's what most would call the "butterfly effect." The entire world commented that they felt and endured this during the COVID-19 pandemic stages.

Limiting us to stay indoors for extended hours and sometimes days on end, not being able to participate with others in our regular daily life routine—we were isolated, cocooned.

Have you ever read or witnessed how a caterpillar must endure this cocoon process in order to transform into something completely different?

This extensive process for a caterpillar is an especially significant one.

The caterpillar must endure this isolation stage to be totally still for a lengthy time in order to transition into something beautiful and exquisite.

We were not aware that this process allowed a lot of us to complete a variety of things—pursue unfinished projects, embark on goals and dreams that benefit one's growth personally and spiritually. Become an entrepreneur or even obtain a college degree. This pandemic allowed you to observe one's real and genuine intent or decipher false encounters and relationships.

It made folks see themselves and others for what their real human makeup consisted of. Some witnessed pain beyond belief from losing loved ones at a very rapid pace. Sizeable amount of relationship connections were either severed or made stronger than prior to being shut in together.

A lot of us, including myself, were isolated away from family and friends.

The experience was rather intense because some areas were free to roam about while the other high COVID-19 case areas where I was staying could only walk, shop, and drive within a ten-mile radius. Wearing a mask for everyone was a must. If caught in public without it, you could be heavily fined or jailed.

The entire country of Kuwait had a curfew every night for months. Airports were closed for almost a year, and folks were stuck out of the country and not allowed back until the Ministry of Health council voted. Some days, I would literally see folks living right across the highway from me who are able to walk around and drive due to their areas not being restricted. It is truly annoying!

The reality of the isolation started to sink in for the majority. It caused so many adverse effects from depression and a high rate of unemployment. Some did not have enough food. Times became very desperate for some, but for me, this was the time that I really connected with myself and my feelings.

I still hadn't processed my divorce fully. I was still playing scenarios in my head of all of the craziness that I, not too long ago, experienced, asking myself questions and digging deep to find the real me.

I was tired of listening to others' negative remarks and comments and allowing their doubts to consume me. I was literally starting to doubt myself. "Was I really good enough?" Sitting still made me face my demons and my shortcomings to come to grips with the thought that I was human and allowed to make mistakes. Somehow, I was deemed to make many more.

Address and confront the very thing that was hindering me. Self-sabotage at its best. Once I peeled back the layers of my onion, I realized that I was a dope-ass queen, living in my truth and accepting things and people as they were and not changing anyone but myself. I will be accountable for her!

When placed into a setting such as this, we must surrender to growth, unknowing of the outcome.

It is almost a "faith thing," a sense of vulnerability of you believing in something that is not tangible but obtainable.

Within this time, I was able to complete a major goal, something that played a huge part in my purpose in this life. I studied and completed my certificate to be a certified life coach from the Say Life Coach Institute.

To some, this is a minor feat. But for me, I finally accepted the challenge that I had put off for years, ultimately answering the nagging that was constantly tugging at me from within, to step into my rite and enter the passage to my purpose and just do it.

The completion of this process would resemble the transition, which would symbolize my growth and expansion. I needed to do this! At that very moment, T.Renee was reintroduced. *How are you doing?* This was such a *huge* accomplishment for me!

Once you truly let go and accept experiencing a metamorphosis of this magnitude, trusting the process, completing the work at hand, and accepting your outcome—transforming your situation and recreating yourself into a brand-new beautiful butterfly—become easier to adjust.

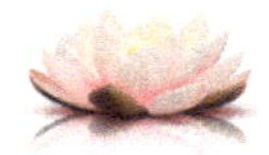

Chapter 5

When Your Gears Strip, Stuck in Neutral (Push to Start)

Don't allow your past or present condition to control you. It's just a process that you're going through to get you to the next level.

—T. D. Jakes

You are getting ready to commute to work. You woke up in such an awesome mood this morning, excited about the day, and you got plenty of rest. You're driving along. Approaching a red light, you go to shift your gears and proceed to stop, and guess what happens? You stop, and your car shuts off and won't start. Now the clutch is stripped.

This darn car had been acting up for a while now. You didn't make the time to get it checked out by your local mechanic. Instead, you put it off. "It can wait, I got more important things to worry about." This my friend is indeed important. It is your transportation to get you to and from work, a vital part of sustaining your lively hood. So what happens next is you decide how you are going to control the narrative.

Of course, we instantly begin to panic, worry, and doubt. "I can't be late again. My boss already warned me this week. How much will it cost to fix?"

In that instance, the good vibes that you were feeling earlier have now turned into a negative one. You must quickly find a way to get back to that good place. You must instantly block the negativity of this situation, which is trying to taint your mindset.

Let's ponder on this for a moment. Fun fact, the advantage of having a manual transmission in your car is this: the clutch controls the connection between the shaft coming from the engine and the shaft which turns the wheels. This means that you have more control in this situation than you assume to have.

You must affirm and tell yourself that there is a good reason for this very thing to be happening. Sometimes we have to remind ourselves about speaking negatively to ourselves or our situation. Remember the tongue is a very powerful tool that can either hinder or help us.

So now let's use our tools on how we can create the solution for this problem. Let's list the key factors on how we can get out of this and get back on track. Instantly, you have agreed to revert back to your positive space. You recalled that you got a clutch, a manual car that, if pushed, can jumpstart on its own. Think of the important pointers in chapter 3 "No Thanks, Keep Your Fear?" You begin to apply them, and at once, you think, *If I can get a little help, the mechanic is only a few blocks away*, and I almost forgot, *We just signed up for triple-A road service*. Problem solved.

Just like that, the experience that seemed undoable and out of our control has now turned into a situation that ended with success due to our thought process and due to realizing that things that are out of our control are just that. It is up to us how we create and handle the outcome.

Sure, we can beat ourselves for not tending to that thing sooner to avoid the mishap, but what if the mishap totally blindsided you? You did not even see the approach of it coming your way. So how do we handle this? First, it is how we process this very thing in our mind, the examples of how it could have been way worse than what is happening right now.

To always know you have options if you care to seek them out and for us to be grateful for being spared and regrouped. Sometimes we are actually placed in situations that help us grow and learn that we are the only ones that can push out the very greatness that is instilled in us. Lastly, sometimes the very thing that will cause difficulty, setback, or adversity can motivate us to do better and be better.

Sometimes the clutch must be stripped to recognize the habit of procrastination. You know the procrastination. The doubt of you not being able to complete the very thing that will catapult you into the awesome person you deemed to be. Now get up, and go get that new clutch. You got work to do!

 Have you ever experienced a situation that was totally out of your control, but your positive thinking changes the ending for it to be something great?

Chapter 6

When We Think We Are Too Special to Be in a Storm

You cannot see in a storm that's why he told
you to walk by faith and not by sight.

—T. D. Jakes

Why me? Why? These are some of the questions we may ask ourselves when bad things happen to us. What did I do to endure or experience this sort of thing or pain? We never know what situations or circumstances have been addressed or destined for us to encounter during our lifetime.

The aftermath of our life situations, trials, and tribulations may cause us a feeling that we should not have been susceptible to it when we are under the impression that we are *too special to be in a storm.*

I had to endure the hardest heartbreak of my mother passing and then getting a divorce after twenty-six years of marriage. Each experience happened within a five-year period. Hands down, this was the most trying season in my life. As I was going through my divorce, it literally felt as if I was grieving death all

28

over again as I did with the loss of my mother. I felt that at that very moment, my life as I had known and grown accustomed to for many years was pretty much over.

This situation took a rough toll on me and my children mentally and physically. It was extremely hard. Drained, exhausted, weary, and tired were the feelings that I experienced in this very trying period in my life.

I had to rely on my spiritual background and belief in the almighty God. I had to know that there was a lesson in this learning and that I had to go through this so-called storm for a reason. During that time, I could not feel nor see anything but chaos, hurt, pain, loneliness, frustration, anger, and depression. Hell, I could go on and on. There were so many emotions rushing in all at once.

I was now in the center of my spiritual tornado, a personal hell, and I wanted out *now*! My life, my family—so many things I could see constantly swirling all around me in my wind tunnel. It seemed so dark and lonely. The abyss was the only thing that would come to my mind. Every day I tried to maintain a smile and laugh while wearing a mask, constantly encouraging and mentoring and motivating others when my cup itself was truly depleted. My soul was crying deep down. I was dying inside, broken. My eyes had lost all the sparkle. The happy that was always present was hidden. My spirit man was in a battle. I was all alone to feel all of this. I wasn't sure how long this would be and if I could or would ever get out of this.

I started to envision myself literally wanting to reach in that storm, come against the indestructible winds, and pull those things down to take back my control and restore my life the way that it was. To take back the things that I had lost and restore some type of normalcy within me.

I had to remind myself that when you reach into a storm, the suction from the very winds that are coming against you can cause you to get sucked in. Tornado winds can reach as high as 300 mph, which can cause something as heavy as a hundred-ton vehicle to be tossed around like a sheet of paper. Even though I wasn't in an actual tornado, the effects felt as though I was.

I was always anxious and not sure of the very outcome.

I prayed and relied on my faith in God to keep me very still. I repeatedly had to maintain my peace of mind and balance with various motivational tools and videos. The love and support from family and friends played a key role in maintaining my sanity as well as learning how to incorporate a positive outlook, reprogramming my mindset, being intentional with my actions, speaking positive affirmations to myself, and trusting the process.

Even though some days were harder than others, I had to visualize the bigger picture of what my future can and could be. That I will pull through this. That the spirit of resilience had been placed in me since birth by my mother (she, too, was a strong queen). To be that exemplified example for my daughters, encouraging them to know that with faith in God, we could and would survive this, and we did!

Sometimes the very thing God strips from us in the storm will lead to bigger and better things that he has in store for us, breaking up the very thing that may be hindering us and holding us up from walking into our God-given purpose.

So remember, sometimes the storm is not to destroy but to actually clear your path for unseen greatness.

Set Boundaries
Stick to them...
Pray and Meditate
Daily...
Start to Learn to
Love and Like You...
CREATE
Daily Rituals and Positive Habits...
Surround Yourself
with Positive People and Places..
Know that YOU
are More than a conqueror...

Progress

Chapter 7

Can You Handle Your Own Accountability and Actions?

You are the only real obstacle in your path to fulfilling it.
—Les Brown

It is so easy to point fingers at others for our mistakes, choices, or mishaps. But when we are faced with conducting our own self-evaluation and taking that long look at our reflection in the mirror, can we handle our own accountability when we wonder who is really staring back?

For example, when you promised yourself for New Year's that your resolution was to go on a diet, or you said that this would be the year that you were going to get focused and leave your dead-end job. Lastly, how about the ongoing toxic love relationship that is clearly going nowhere?

We encounter so much during our lifetime, and sometimes, we do not even recognize that we ourselves have been exposed to traumatic events in our childhood.

We think that if we only experience situations where we were mentally and physically abused, it is the only life-changing interactions that we encounter that may damage us.

These things indeed can emotionally scar our very being, our inner man. But there are so many other instances that some of us witness and experience that are left to process and harbor in our subconscious to be forgotten. Instances that are buried, but sadly, they rise.

They show up in our relationships and our day-to-day interactions with others—being attracted to broken people and broken circumstances and not addressing or holding the very situation's accountability.

Sometimes we may have to stop and ask ourselves, How do we defer what consist of a healthy relationship? How can we set boundaries and address often-overlooked red flags? And lastly, how to regain our self-worth fully and learn how to let go when a situation is no longer adding value to our lives.

While growing up, for the most part, my mother gave me a loving home and taught me morals and values (how to give love), but she never taught us (me and my siblings) how to avoid toxic love and toxic situations.

She would always say, "Show love like Christ showed us." But what Mom should have been teaching, instilling, and showing us were examples of being in healthy relationships and what that looks and feels like, showing us the realness of the good, the bad, and the terrible. But she never experienced this very thing herself, she fell trapped so many times to broken promises and the heartache of false love.

I will never forget the time when my parents went through their divorce. This was my first experience of heartbreak. I was a daddy's girl, and now at seven years old, I will have to experience and harbor the memories of not seeing him or even getting to hug or hold him. It was outright devastating. This, my friend, is a form of trauma.

So many of us will carry and implement its effects throughout our adult lives in many other scenarios. My marriage ended pretty much the same way, knowing that we were both broken, harboring hurt, negative energy, and pain from our pasts. We never acquired healing from our past experiences nor did we learn and implement our love languages. This alone is an important key factor in creating and keeping any loving, lasting, and healthy relationship. In some part, we were unequally yoked, as some would say, but God allowed our union for a reason, and just for that I'm grateful to have encountered it.

Life is so funny. Again the things that we speak and put into the atmosphere can be very powerful and life-changing. I always told myself that I would never end up being single, alone, or another divorcee statistic, but God knew that this, too, was necessary for me and my daughter's growth. If they were ever to be faced with a toxic or unhealthy relationship, they would have the tools to empower themselves with strength, courage, and self-confidence to require better.

I encouraged my daughters to find their own way of healing from my damaging situation. I advocated to always pour into themselves and learn how to genuinely love yourself first.

I will also encourage them to utilize and welcome therapy. So many of us scoff or even laugh at this form of practice and think that it is useless. But having a neutral party who will not place judgment can greatly lift the burden and help one to release the guilt, shame, and confusion that have often been misplaced.

The rule in therapy is not to connect to you and not give judgment but give a clear opinion from someone outside looking inward. This will allow you to unload freely and start the healing process and lift the weight that has unnoticeably been carried. This will stop the cycle of unhealthy relationships and allow you to experience the goodness and love that you deserve.

In no way do I regret my divorce. I shared great memories and experiences. Even though my outcome may have seemed similar to my parents divorcing, this factor needed to be played out in my life, in order for me to share my story today.

I have accepted my accountability and have focused on my healing so that I will not repeat the cycle for without the union of my parents or me going through and enduring those situations, I would not be here. I would not be T.Renee.

Reflection: Have you experience a situation where you had to confront yourself and take accountability for your actions? How was your outcome?

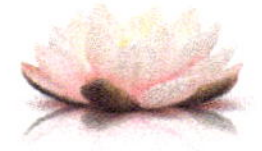

Chapter 8

Late On Arrival, but Didn't Miss the Show. Waiting On the When

Your beginning never dictates your destination.

—Tyler Perry

Have you ever been in a scenario where you planned a special night out?

For months you have been researching something fun to do. Suddenly you hear on the radio that your favorite director, Tyler Perry, with one of his famous plays would be coming to your city. Oh, snap! He will be here next month. Instantly you go to planning mode in your head. "I have to research the dates and ticket prices. I want to get a good seat." After reviewing the tickets, you notice that the front row is completely sold out, and the only ones on sale are the balcony top on the second row. You say to yourself, *It doesn't matter. I'm going.* You book and pay for your seat. The countdown now begins.

You are so excited you start marking the dates off your calendar. Thirty days will be here in no time. Day by day it is getting closer to the play date.

Excited you tell family and friends you're going to the play, and you begin to get your outfit together. You got a sitter for the kids. You are ready. Finally, the day of the event has arrived. You even left early from work.

You are thinking to yourself, *This will truly be a night to remember. I haven't treated myself out in a while*, assuring yourself that you're going to have fun. You get dressed. You are sharp. Face beat to the gods. Hair done. Nails done. Everything done as Swish Beats would say.

You take that last glance in the full-length mirror to give the final approval. "Yes, ma'am. You are ready!" You are about to leave, heading out the front door, and it starts raining cats and dogs. It looks like a repeat of Hurricane Katrina, and she is at full speed, pulling out all the shots! You do a mad dash to the car but are careful not to get wet or fall. You slam the car door and think, *Why of all nights?* As sheets of rain hit your car while you are driving, the rain is pouring down so hard you barely can see the vehicles in front of you.

You look at your watch, the play started over an hour ago, and you are literally around the corner. The traffic is now at a standstill, bumper to bumper, because of the horrible weather. "Ugh, of all days, why today?" You say out loud, "I do not want to miss a single thing. His plays are always sold out!"

So as you inch thirty miles per hour through traffic, you begin to get anxious, *waiting on the when*: "When will I get there?" "When will the rain stop?" "I am going to miss the play!" "This can't be happening to me!" You are beyond upset and getting a tad bit frustrated. The negative seeds are being planted by your words and your thought process, and your whole mood is shot.

When you finally reach the venue and park the car with the valet, you quickly start speed walking to the lobby. The play was scheduled to start at 8:00 p.m. It's 9:30 p.m.! As you head to the theater's main doors, you start to look around and admire the beautiful decor in the corridors. Suddenly the negative energy is melting, and you are feeling a sense of relief, "You made it!"

As the usher smiles and warmly greets you, she takes your ticket. Before she proceeds to escort you to your seat, she mentions that due to the weather you have the option of seating closer to the stage, in the front row section.

You think to yourself, *Heck yeah! Blessing number one.* You quickly nod yes, and off you guys go b-lining toward the stage. The whole time you are walking, you are thinking, *Man, this is so cool, these are the seats I really wanted!* As you sit in your new assigned seat, you notice that you are two rows over from Tamala Mann, who is in the audience with other celebrity guests.

Oh my god! I definitely would not have seen her from my purchased seats, you said to yourself. *This cannot be happening!* Lastly, you start looking around, and as you are waiting, you noticed that the play hasn't started yet. The curtain is still down, and *you didn't miss one thing from the curtain call or the show*!

When things happen beyond our control, we must take a moment and tell ourselves that maybe there is a reason that this is happening. Maybe we are avoiding or being protected from something, like a mishap or an accident. Maybe God is aligning something special for us.

His perfect timing requires patience on our end. We are so quick to question and rush what we think is the right time or thing, not knowing what God really has in store for us! When we think that we have missed the mark on embarking and manifesting our dreams, destiny, our opportunities for growth, expanding our territories, or success, just remember that in God's timing, He has everything perfectly aligned for us. What is for you in your season, you will obtain and have it.

God will open doors and windows that no man can close. Every blessing that has your name on it will be presented to you in due time. So remember in your due season, you will not miss a single thing, not even the curtain call. You can sit back and enjoy the entire play.

Reflection: Name a time when you were supposed to experience a special event, and because of unforeseen circumstances, you thought that you were going to miss it but instead was blessed from it.

Chapter 9

When the Shedding Is Necessary, Letting Go and Accepting the Glow-Up!

We delight in the beauty of the butterfly, but rarely admit
the changes it has gone through to achieve that beauty.
—Maya Angelou

"Trust the process." Uttering those very words is easier said than done, especially from someone who has never experienced or who has never been through this kind of situation or loss. The transition from being a wife of twenty-six years to soon-to-be newly single was surely taking place, trying so hard to stay contained, remain occupied, and just function from day to day. I had lost my job doing this process, and the divorce was in full swing ahead. I needed to get my mind and thoughts together to accept this new season. I truly was in the so-called "sunken place."

I was going out every night with my crew, assisting my dear sister with her company on the weekends. I was doing anything to stay busy and not ponder on what was really going on within me.

I was trying to mask the serious trauma that I was enduring to learn how to cope with my soon-to-be new norm.

During this time, one of my sisters reached out to me and offered me a position in Kuwait. Heck yeah, I accepted the job. This was a perfect opportunity to escape my current situation with a clean slate and start over to literally break out and divert all of the foolery, chaos, negative atmosphere, and distractions that seem to be looming all around me.

I felt like I couldn't shake the feeling of uneasiness and doubt. I was ready for my new change to get my happiness and peace of mind back! Surely I would miss all of my family and friends, but this move was absolutely necessary, and it couldn't have presented itself at a better time! I started to prepare for my move, and I got ready to embark on my next chapter, working abroad back in Kuwait. This was not my first rodeo working in this foreign land. In fact, my first time ever leaving the United States was right before Hurricane Katrina in 2006. My family transitioned here before the major storm hit New Orleans. We had lost everything that we had ever owned, literally starting all over. Even though we had lost it all, it was a golden opportunity to rebuild our entire life, better than it was before. This was an unforeseen blessing, a lifetime adventure to live and work in the Middle East.

So for me, to come back to this place was very familiar territory. This was my second home. I had been here prior for almost eleven years with my family. When I arrived, it felt like I was in a dream, walking in a fog, not feeling a bit real.

So many memories came rushing back in, from me and my girls first touching down at the airport, to how we experienced the heat index, which was so hot that it literally took our breath away, to even my own mother coming to work here. I had to pause, take a deep breath, and exhale. This was really happening, but this time, with only me.

Everything happened so fast from shuffling from the terminal going through Customs and finally baggage claims. It still didn't hit me that I was indeed back, but this was real for sure. It took a moment for me to soak it all in, realizing for the first time in years I was on my own. I was received by my new colleagues at the front of the airport. Creating that bond of getting to know your new battle buddy seemed natural. We finally loaded the company van and proceeded to head to our living quarters. I was still moving in slow motion almost in a dream-like state. Trying to process the divorce, learning before I left to travel to Kuwait that my ex had remarried not even two months after the divorce was finalized, and working back in Kuwait without my family. Trust me, the load of this burden weighed a ton, and it was on my shoulders, heavy as hell! One thing that helped me remain positive about the transition back to Kuwait was all the family and friends who were still residing there for many years after we left in 2014.

I knew once I saw them that I could start to rebuild my self-confidence and self-worth again, but this, too, will take time. Seeing their friendly faces would be very welcoming and therapeutic.

I was excited to hug and talk with the sisters from another mother who really helped and encouraged me through this process. My day ones!

But once we started to reminisce on the old times, when I was here prior for eleven years with my family, they, too, knew that I had changed. That I wasn't the same woman that was here many years ago. That my current dynamic had forced me to become isolated and slightly withdrawn to reevaluate people and see things differently.

My sisters felt as though they, too, were going through this with me because of the close bond that we had shared throughout the years. They felt the pain and hurt as I told them about the events that I, my children, and grandchildren had endured and witnessed. They, too, were in total shock, and we would just sit and cry to witness firsthand that the vibrant spirit that I once had was not being seen and how this transition affected so many lives. Tears are cleansing for the soul, but I had wailed and cried so much back stateside that I didn't want folks to pity nor feel sorry for me. I was experiencing the same things and places here in Kuwait again alone and making new memories without my family. I found myself being isolated from my friends due to our different work schedules and folks just having a life. Everything definitely had changed.

I had accepted my new change. With that mindset, I, too, started to implement my new way of thinking, a new way of talking to myself, affirming that I would not allow this situation to harden my heart nor close my heart to love again—to love me first!

This feeling went on for the first year of me coming back. I had to realize that God had placed me here, back in this familiar place and space, to remove me and make me uncomfortable for a season to grow and allow me to get used to being by myself, to enjoy my own company, to start my healing process, to learn how to forgive, how not to continue to blame myself, and to accept and love the soon-to-be new me. Trust me, it was tough!

But my faith remained strong and unwavering because for once, I was at peace!

This process needed to be achieved, He needed to remold me to show me how to pour back into me for my happiness for me to learn who and whose I was. That I was still blessed and highly favored. That I was a queen. He remolded me so I would know that going through this, I was never alone or had been alone. God had been there the entire time until I realize this the shedding of the old me was starting to take place, and I was now ready for the glow-up!

"Therefore if any man be in Christ, he is a new creature; old things are passed away, behold, all things are become new" (2 Corinthians 5:17).

Reflection: Have you ever experienced a situation where you had to be isolated to embrace your next season of growth and transformation? What tools did you implement for this?

Manifest

Chapter 10

When You Are Startled by the Glass Door

Be not afraid of growing slowly, be afraid of standing still.
—Chinese Proverb

It is a beautiful Saturday afternoon, and you have decided that you had been cooped up in the house all week. You wanted some fresh air and to do a little shopping, so you headed to the mall. While leaving the mall, your cellphone rang, it was your best friend telling you about her date last night. She was giving you all the tea, how he was handsome, how the conversation was amazing, and how she would be going on another date with him this Saturday night.

You were so engulfed with the conversation, and it was a juicy one too. You were smiling and laughing, and you scanned around for the exit while still talking to your friend. Not paying attention, you didn't see the "Enter" sign on the automatic door due to you being distracted and engulfed in your conversation.

You continued to walk forward, heading toward the exit, and *bam*! You walked right into the glass door! Not only are you startled but you were also embarrassed because your hitting the glass made a loud thump sound, which echoed and caused folks to stop and see what happened.

As you picture this scenario, it is crazy how we can miss the glass door that is right in front of us. The glass was so clear that it seemed invisible, but it was not. Just like when we go through life's situations and circumstances that cause us to be startled and stopped, that puts a pause on our goals, dreams, and even our purpose if we are not careful. What stopped you from realizing the glass door was the distraction of being on the cell phone. We may deal with all kinds of things that may distract or deter us from focusing on the things that we are destined to be or do.

We can sabotage ourselves with seeds of negativity and doubt, which are planted in our mindset and which can cause us to think that we may not be good enough or deserving of greatness. Most of the time we have many great ideas and concepts that we may lose focus on because we are distracted by family, friends, loved ones, our children…the list goes on and on. Some will take their visions and creativity straight to the grave. Experiencing this pandemic and being in lockdown in my apartment for five months and not being able to go outside of a ten-mile perimeter really gave me a different perspective of life and what truly matters! Losing so many friends and their family members at a rapid rate due to this really caused everyone to take a step back and reanalyze what really matters. Tomorrow is never promised, and due to this pandemic, this has been proven to be true.

Not being able to enjoy the simple pleasures of walking down the street to the beach because it was on the opposite side of the street that was not considered quarantined was an eye-opener.

From that day forward, I have learned to seize every moment, tell folks I love them often, work on myself and my purpose, and heck, write this book.

Even though life may throw us a curveball, it is up to us to regroup, pay attention to the things that are happening around us, and stop being distracted, especially by the glass door.

*Reflection: What is your example of being startled by the glass door? What **steps** did you revise to get back on track?*

Chapter 11

Effects Of Odorless Gases—Allowing Negative Folks in Your Circle

Stay away from negative people, they have
a problem for every solution.

—Albert Einstein

Have you ever been in a situation where you thought the people around you (your circle of close friends or family) were rooting for you, but instead they're your silent enemies, plotting and giving off signals of jealousy, envy, and negative thoughts, wishing that you fail at all the things you inspire to achieve and be?

These same folks who will encourage, smile in your face, and want to be around you are secretly hating on you. You'll ask why.

When you accepted the process of healing, your new role in your chapter, and your newly-found purpose, things that were once hidden deep inside you (traumatic things that you once experienced) changed you.

After experiencing any life-changing situation, we tend to view things in a different manner. It may even cause us to outgrow certain circumstances, places, and people.

When people witness this new transition and transformation of your growth, it may intimidate and cause folks to respond and interact differently.

Some may not congratulate your success of pushing forward to be better than when you were in your situation, especially if they are dealing with a similar or non-positive situation.

Remember, everyone that you encounter may not be able to process your new way of thinking and new way of responding. It is an adjustment for everyone.

But keep in mind that your energy and peace are particularly important. Protect them at all costs. If folks are constantly giving negative comments and vibes, you do not have to subject yourself to their negative energy. Remember, your mindset is processing things differently.

How you process and proceed with this change will continue to grow and remind you on being mindful of the new circle and life you will create. Just like carbon monoxide, it is a silent, odorless, and tasteless gas that if consumed in large amounts in a contained space can and will kill you.

You may encounter people that will give you all sorts of advice on how you should handle your new circumstance. Never accept advice from someone who is trying to show you how to tie up your tennis shoes when they never owned a pair.

Setting and Crushing Your Goals........

You are now in a phase where you have completed your previous lists of Daily and Weekly Goals. Stay in the Habit of always challenging yourself and to create more Goals when completed.

Be Intentional with Self-Love........
Take Time for YOU...Period

Learn new ways to express Your Emotions and Feelings........
Always find Creative ways to aid in your path to healing.

Chapter 12

When Someone Trying to Add Salt to Your **Sugar**

Jealousy is a miserable feeling. It means you
aspire to something that you cannot have.
—Sophia Loren

Have you ever been in a situation where you walked into a room full of folks—for example, a meeting, a work conference, a party, or a break room? You recognize some of the people in the room but the majority don't. As you scan the room and smile at the ones that are pleasantly acknowledging you, you see the others that are engaging in conversation, but you feel the cold stares, the hot coals of negative words, and glances. So you zoom in like a photographic lens, and there you spot them, the endangered species called the hater. They are literally rolling their eyes, faces scrunched up, upset because you have entered the building. You then ask yourself, "What's wrong with them?" You don't even know them, but it's something within you that has totally disrupted their spirit. This is what you may call "someone trying to add salt to your sugar."

Have you ever met someone that gets mad or upset because *you* are in a positive mood or doing well in life or complimenting others? What do you do when you encounter the Debbie Downers or the Negative Nancy and you literally can feel the shift of the atmosphere when these types of people enter the room, literally sucking the life out of the room? Well, it's our responsibility for the energy that we give and the ones that we engage in. Either it will add value to our situation or our lives or take away from it.

You must know that it's your responsibility as the gatekeeper of your spiritual/inner man to guard your peace of mind and inner joy at all times, at all costs. It's up to you to know that it's important for you not to allow folks to speak ill will or negative situations in your life. As I said in the beginning, the tongue is the smallest but the most powerful tool that we possess.

It's important for us to make sure that we are arming ourselves with the proper tools to stay focused—healthy eating, feeding our bodies with good foods, maintaining a positive mindset, and learning to be all-around balanced. I know it's so hard these days between the long work week, stress with day-to-day life situations, on top of inflation, but know that this is temporary and shall too pass!

The things that God allows us to go through, no matter how big or small the situation maybe is a test, are teaching us a lesson in something that will ultimately make us better. You may never know why someone may or may not like you, just because "you are you." All you can do is continue to show up every day as the *best* version of yourself! Continue to be that positive life force that others may need to recharge and make it through the day, for you to be that light that shines in the darkest of times, for you to be the result of your testimony as the winner God created you to be!

Remember that salt and sugar may look the same, but trust that when you taste them, they are totally different. Always be the sugar, and use salt for your food.

Reflection: What are some of the methods or tactics you use to maintain a positive attitude, atmosphere, or energy?

Chapter 13

When You're Blessed to Get the Extra Burger

Don't just count your blessings. Be the
blessing other people count on.

—Anonymous

It had been an extremely busy day, all day. You literally worked
through lunch and completely missed breakfast this morning
because of a deadline for an important client that was due over
an hour ago. You pushed through and finally finished and sub-
mitted your finished product, and the client emailed you back.
They were very happy with the results, and you gathered your
stuff to head home.

On your way home, you saw your favorite burger joint.
You were exhausted, and going inside to order was definitely
out of the question. So you entered the drive-through. And the
lady asked through the intercom, "Welcome! May I take your
order, please?" Trust the menu had been going through your
mind all day, so you knew exactly what you want. "Combo
number 7 please," you responded. Combo number 7 was a
double-patty burger with cheese and all the fixings. Medium

seasoned fries with a coke. You drove to the next window and paid for your order.

As you patiently waited for your order because you wanted all the items to be fresh, you envisioned how good all this would taste, being that you were famished. The lady opened the drive-thru window and handed you your order as you drove off; the smells were so potent that it was filling the whole car with the pleasant aroma that you had already envisioned. You pulled over because you knew that if you waited till you got home, which was over an hour away, the food wouldn't taste the same. You reached into your bag to check your order and realized you got "blessed with an *extra burger*"? Small unexpected blessings that we may receive when we least expect them.

Sometimes God blesses us when we least expect it. When we are going through hardship or difficulties, he reminds us that he is always there; and that if we maintain the faith of a mustard seed, he will always show us his wonders and grace! I know this to be a proven fact of what he has done and brought me through.

When I was at my lowest, God was there; when I seemed to go down to the dark abyss and couldn't get out, he was there. When folks talked about me, disregarded me, didn't believe in me, he was there! For that alone, I will always remind myself and pray to remain humble, thankful, and grateful!

I have gone through things in my life that only he and I will ever know, and I know that the enemy has tried to take my life a few times, but the God I serve is bigger; and as long as I serve and walk in my purpose in this life, he will continue to cover me.

This book was a long time coming, and I'm so glad that he allowed me to complete this by my fifty-first birthday. Never take anyone or anything for granted; life is not promised nor tomorrow will be given. Know that you are remarkable, awesome, great, more than a conquer, originally made, blessed, and highly favored! Continue to work and heal yourself because every day can be a test; it's on how you pass it! Be blessed and enjoy your extra burger. Alwayz, T.Renee.

*Reflection: Name a time when you received an unexpected blessing or gift or something that happened that caused you to be **extra** thankful for that act.*

About the Author

Tameca Renee is a New Orleans native who is currently working in Kuwait, Middle East, as an MWR (Morale, Welfare, and Recreation) entertainment supervisor, coordinating, planning, and executing logistical support for the military troops abroad with live entertainment and events. She is a certified positivity life coach through "The Say Life" Coach Institute founded by Elyssa Lassiter. Her hobbies are world traveling, enjoying great food, and making awesome life experiences in the process. She is always grateful to be loving and living life to the fullest.

www.ingramcontent.com/pod-product-compliance
Lightning Source LLC
Chambersburg PA
CBHW040157160726
48006CB00014B/1793